MARTIAL ARTS CHARACTER EDUCATION LESSON PLANS FOR CHILDREN

A COMPLETE 16-WEEK CURRICULUM FOR
TEACHING CHARACTER VALUES AND LIFE
SKILLS IN YOUR MARTIAL ART SCHOOL

MIKE MASSIE

MODERN DIGITAL PUBLISHING

MARTIAL ARTS CHARACTER EDUCATION LESSON PLANS FOR CHILDREN

A Complete 16-Week Curriculum for Teaching Character Values and Life Skills in Your Martial Art School

Mike Massie

Modern Digital Publishing
Austin, Texas

Modern Digital Publishing

P.O. Box 682

Dripping Springs, TX 78620

www.MartialArtsBusinessDaily.com

Ordering Information:

Quantity sales. Special discounts are available on quantity purchases by corporations, associations, and others. For details, contact the "Special Sales Department" at the address above.

Martial Arts Character Education Lesson Plans for Children / Mike Massie. —2nd ed. ISBN 978-0-9896683-2-3

"Train up a child in the way he should go: and when he is old, he will not depart from it."

- Proverbs 22:6

INTRODUCTION:

WHAT THIS CHARACTER EDUCATION PROGRAM WILL DO FOR YOUR MARTIAL ART SCHOOL

I'll be the first to admit it—this program is deceptively simple. However, that's exactly the way I designed it, because the last thing I want to do is to complicate the business of running a martial art school. However, no matter how simple this character development program is to learn and execute, I did not create it in some overnight burst of inspiration...

Instead it took me almost two decades to refine and hone the lessons in this book. That's two decades of doing mat chats in up to twenty kid's classes a week, night after night, year after year. And, I kept teaching these same lessons each night, refining the message and delivery until I ended up with what you hold in your hands now.

So, why would I do that? Why teach the same lessons year after year after year? Why not just give up on it and move on to the next shiny new object that just released at the latest martial arts business convention, like most other instructors would do?

Because, quite simply - this program works.

It works to turn skeptical parents into raving fans. It works to turn school teachers who are jaded on bringing martial arts instructors into their schools into enthusiastic evangelists for your cause. It works to get a buzz going in your community about your school.

And most of all, it works for helping kids learn right from wrong, and to develop the courage and self-confidence to choose what is right in their daily lives.

For me, this program is much more than just another martial arts business resource. It is the heart and soul of my children's programs and it is also the essence of my martial arts and moral philosophy. I sincerely hope that what you and your students learn from these pages blesses their lives and your studio as you share these lessons with them.

I know for a fact that teaching this program has blessed mine.

Sincerely,

Mike Massie

Author, *Small Dojo Big Profits*

P.S. - And yes, I realize that I could have easily sold this program for ten times the price you purchased it for or more. *I'm fully aware that others are licensing their character development programs and curricula for thousands of dollars a year.* But, I'm more concerned with helping school owners succeed than I am with lining my pockets. And, I sincerely believe in the power of this program, so I want to get it into as many hands as possible. I strongly advise that you do not let the comparatively low price fool you into believing that there's little value here, because the benefits you'll receive from implementing this program in your studio are immeasurable. This program <u>will</u> bring you **higher student retention** and make you a rock star in your community. Use it wisely.

1

WHY SHOULD YOU CARE ABOUT TEACHING CHARACTER DEVELOPMENT TO CHILDREN?

You might think martial arts studios that focus on teaching character lessons to kids are just one step short of a romper room. You might also assume that the only martial arts schools that focus on this are just strip mall McDojos that teach character values in lieu of good solid martial arts. Yet, if you walk into many of the most successful martial arts schools and mixed martial arts gyms in the country and listen in on what they're teaching in their child-age classes, you'll find that the most successful studios place a strong emphasis on teaching character values to kids.

These studios are successful for a reason, and I believe it relates directly to teaching positive character values to the children in their programs. You may disagree, but my 20 years experience plus in teaching kids martial arts tells me different. And, I can name off a laundry list of successful martial arts instructors who would agree with me.

Then again, if you're reading this there's a strong

chance that you realize the importance of teaching kids character values in this day and age. It doesn't take a child psychologist to see that the world is a very different place from what it was 50 or 60 years ago, or to see that the massive media exposure to sex and violence is taking a huge toll on our children and society as a whole. Today, kids are exposed to more sex and violence at an earlier age than at any previous time in history, and we are seeing the results of this exposure play out in the lives of our children.

Let's look at some statistics to put this in perspective:

- The aggravated assault rate went up from around 60 per 100,000 in 1957, to over 440 per 100,000 by the mid-90's
- The *Journal of the American Medical Association* says that, "the introduction of television in the 1950's caused a subsequent doubling of the homicide rate... if, hypothetically, television technology had never been developed, there would today be 10,000 fewer homicides each year in the United states, 70,000 fewer rapes, and 700,000 fewer injurious assaults"
- The number of violent acts the average American child sees on television by age 18 is 200,000; the number of murders witnessed by children on T.V. by age 18 is 16,000
- Children are thought to behave differently after viewing violent acts and become desensitized to the suffering of others, be more fearful of the

world around them, and to show increased
aggression towards others

By and large, parents feel overwhelmed by the task of protecting their children from the constant onslaught of negative images in the media, and they're looking for ways to help their children grow up as well-adjusted and happy members of society.

And this is where you come in; by offering a values-based character development curriculum as part of your overall martial arts program, you can offer parents something their children won't get anywhere else. That is, you can offer them a powerful positive influence in their lives, and a positive role model their children respect who can deliver important lessons that will stay with them for the rest of their lives.

If you don't think that parents who find out that you offer such a program won't line up around the block to get their child into your classes, then you have never witnessed the power of implementing such a program in a martial art studio. Not only that, but offering such a program elevates you from the role of a mere "coach" to that of a valued expert influencing the lives of hundreds of children in your community. Finally, the personal satisfaction you will receive from knowing you're having a positive impact in your community is invaluable and beyond measure.

If all of this fails to convince you, perhaps you should consider avoiding teaching children altogether. Granted, you can simply teach physical skills to kids, and do so without ever offering anything of a more philosophical and moral depth in your classes; that's your choice.

However, doing so will make you seem as nothing more important to parents than the typical volunteer soccer or baseball coach. The role you choose to take in your community is ultimately your choice; what you have here before you is a means of both elevating your position in your community, as well as a way to impact the lives of hundreds of children in lasting and meaningful way. Which will you choose?

What This Book Is Designed To Provide

As with every martial arts business resource I provide in the *Small Dojo Big Profits* line of products, this system is designed to be implemented with a minimal time investment, while still providing maximum impact and benefits to your studio and students.

While I am aware that there are extensive (and expensive) subscription programs out there that provide lengthy and complex monthly lesson plans, based on my two decades plus experience teaching children, I honestly don't think you need them. For almost twenty years I've taught these same 32 character development lessons and variations on those lessons, over and over again. You might think that it would get repetitive, but the more I teach these lessons, the more I find something new to teach about each character value and life lesson.

What's even more surprising is that I've found the repetition of these lessons to be incredibly beneficial for the children I've taught. Following my system, you're only going to repeat each lesson once every eight months or so. This is just enough repetition to remind children who have already heard a lesson before of things they may have forgotten or missed the first time around, but not so much that the lessons become less stimulating or less interesting.

So, what this program provides is a very simple, easy to teach, easily prepared system of 16 weekly character development mat chats, with each week divided into two lessons per week for a total of 32 lessons. Again, these lessons are easy to teach and they don't require extensive preparation to use. You should be able to take simple notes for each day and review each lesson in under five minutes, and be still able to teach the entire lesson with confidence with only minimal pre-class preparation time.

TEACHING CHARACTER DEVELOPMENT
IN THE MARTIAL ARTS

The concept of teaching character values has become nearly synonymous with teaching martial arts. For better or for worse, since the original Karate Kid movie was released the public has held the image of benevolent, peace-loving, slightly cantankerous Mr. Miyagi to be the measure by which all children's martial arts instructors should be measured.

But just how important is it really to the success of your school that you teach positive values such as courtesy to your students? Isn't it enough to simply follow traditional rituals of bowing and calling instructors "sir", "ma'am", or sensei? Is it really necessary to do more?

THE BIRTH of Martial Arts Character Development Programs for Children

The concept of "teaching benefits" has been around for a

while in the martial arts industry. I believe it actually started right after The Karate Kid released, when martial arts instructors suddenly realized that parents who brought their children to them actually expected the instructors to teach them more than the skills of physical violence.

Sure, you can call it "self-defense" if you like, but without internal tempering the external skills of the martial arts are merely weaponry in the hands of any person. Just as a firearm knows no inherent ethics or morality, neither do the physical skills of the martial arts bear any of these traits either, no matter how much we wish to romanticize the arts we practice.

Parents were quick to pick up on this; I would imagine that it started the first time a kid used what they learned in class at school and the parents got a call from the principal. I can hear the parents' complaint now: "I wanted you to teach him to be like Ralph Macchio, not those Cobra-Kai kids!" And, I'm sure the first instructor who heard this complaint soon realized that the gravy train was going to leave the station if he didn't start instilling some character values into the kids in his classes.

Enter the Mat Chat

But here's the thing; if just modeling courteous behavior isn't enough (and any parent knows this to be the case) then how do you teach these lessons within the span of a 45-60 minute martial arts class? Thus, the concept of the mat chat was born, the mat chat being a specific time (roughly 3-5 minutes) set aside during each martial arts class to teach a brief character values or life skills lesson.

By having a specified time set aside during each class when students are verbally instructed on the virtues of courtesy and so forth, not only are such lessons reinforced regularly, but also parents who are watching classes from the sidelines actually get to witness the lessons being imparted.

As you can imagine, this can have a profound impact on student retention rates, as well as rates of student referrals to your studio. Not only that, but teaching these character values also provides a deeper and more profound sense of meaning to the martial arts instruction you provide. So, not only does it improve your bottom line, it also provides you, the instructor, with a deeper sense of personal fulfillment from teaching martial arts as well.

THE FLIP-SIDE of Teaching Courtesy as a Profession

However apparent the financial and social benefits of teaching character development programs might be, there is a flip-side to doing so that you need to be aware of before you start teaching them in your school. And that is, you'll automatically be held to a higher standard by virtue of the very lessons you are attempting to instill in your students.

Thus, the burden also remains with you, the instructor, to make certain you can live up to what you're teaching in your mat chats, because certainly you will be held up to the standards you expect from your students.

In other words, you can't be a hypocrite. If you teach courtesy and other values to your students, you need to take a good long look inside and at how you conduct yourself in your interactions with others, and honestly evaluate whether or not you're living up to your lessons. Believe me, if you put yourself forth in your community as a person who is a role model for children, someone is always going to be watching your every move in public.

- Lose your cool and flip someone off in traffic? It'll probably be one of the parents who bring their children to your class...
- Snap at the person who mixed up your order at that restaurant? You don't recognize him, but his nephews and nieces attend your school...
- Plan to get sauced at the town festival? Don't even think about it...
- Refuse to pay a bill with a local vendor? All her clients are likely to be your clients as well, and people talk...

My point here is that as a profession that has evolved into this sub-niche of teaching character development programs for children, we need to hold ourselves to a higher standard, or we risk losing our credibility as a profession entirely.

The Importance of Modeling Character Values

So, my advice to you is that you model the courtesy you're teaching your younger students both inside and outside the dojo. For many of you who are reading this, this is no news to you. That's likely because you've already internalized all those lessons you've been teaching your child-age students, and most likely you did so long before you opened your studio.

But for others of you who are reading this right now, you have a decision to make. Will you continue to preach courtesy and self-control on week nights, and then let it all hang out when you think no one is looking? Or, will you make a commitment to bettering yourself for the sake of your business and your students' welfare?

Look, we all screw up on occasion. Whether it's losing our cool with someone, or being short with your kids or spouse, or "forgetting" to pay a bill on time... but the thing is, we need to hold ourselves to a higher standard, before we make a mistake that can have a lasting negative impact on the most impressionable students we have.

TEACHING CHARACTER VALUES TO CHILDREN

Teaching character values to children can be both rewarding and challenging for martial arts instructors. It is rewarding because over time you'll be able to see the positive changes in your students, and you'll also hear about it when you receive positive feedback from parents and school teachers. However, it can also be challenging, because you're essentially trying to teach abstract concepts to children, and this can be difficult, especially with younger age groups.

When approaching the task of teaching children character values, you must first understand the developmental stages of cognitive growth that children go through:

- **The Pre-operational Stage:** This is the period of growth that occurs between age two and age six when a child learns to use language. In this stage kids cannot understand or use concrete logic, they can't mentally manipulate information, and they're unable to take the point of view of other people.

- **The Concrete Operational Stage:** Between ages seven and eleven children develop a greater command of mental operations. At this stage they start thinking logically about concrete events, but they still have difficulty understanding abstract or hypothetical concepts.
- **The Formal Operational Stage:** The growth period between ages twelve to adulthood is when young people begin to develop the ability to think about abstract concepts. At this stage they develop skills such as deductive reasoning, logical thought, and systematic planning.

Can you see how this can complicate the task of teaching children such abstract concepts as honor, integrity, and perseverance? While teens and even older children may readily grasp such concepts, younger children will be unable to internalize your lessons unless you are able to teach them in concrete and personal terms. What exactly do I mean by this?

An Example of Teaching Character Values to Children

With children in your younger age groups (for most studios this will be ages 4-6 and 7-12) the liberal use of *practical examples* and *simple language* are necessary for teaching character values. This means you have to show kids what each value is and what it would mean to use it, or not. And, you have to consistently use language that is easy for a child to understand.

For example, let's say I was teaching a lesson on honesty. I would begin by introducing the word, having written it on the whiteboard before class:

"Class, the Word of the Week is <u>honesty</u>. Who can tell me what that means?"

By asking a question, I am encouraging the students to engage. However, not many students will be able to provide a concrete response that succinctly describes what honesty is; even so, I'll field several of their answers, using praise to coach and reinforce their efforts.

Next, I'll respond to the answer that most closely approximates the definition. At this point I'll write the abbreviated "formal definition" on the whiteboard, telling the class that "this is what the dictionary says honesty is":

"Honesty: Being truthful"

At this point, I'll expand on the abbreviated formal definition by asking another question to illustrate the *opposite* of what the term means:

"So, is being truthful telling the truth, or lying?"

Every kid can relate to lying and telling the truth, because most kids have been taught from the time they could speak that telling the truth is important.

At this point, I'll introduce an example:

"Okay, so honesty is telling the truth. Let's pretend your mom made some cookies but she told you that you couldn't have one until after dinner. But, you really wanted a cookie right now, so you snuck one from the cookie jar. When your mom

asked you if you snuck a cookie, you told her 'no'. Is that honesty?"

Don't be surprised that some kids will get this confused at this point. That's okay. What we're trying to do is help the kids understand the lesson by giving them a concrete example that illustrates the central theme.

"Of course not! That would be lying. So, what should we do instead? That's right, we should tell the truth. Very good!"

For your youngest students, this is about as far as you'll be able to go with this concept. However, older children in your 7-12 year old classes may benefit from taking the concept further. For example, in your next class you might discuss why it's also dishonest to take things that aren't yours. This concept will be lost on younger kids, but older kids will more easily grasp how stealing relates to a lack of honesty.

Using This Pattern During Mat Chats

I believe at this point you can see how important it is to introduce these concepts through engagement, examples, and interactive coaching. The example I provide above is also illustrative of how you should teach your mat chats in class.

Let's review the steps I followed above to clarify how you should teach your mat chats:

1. Write the "Word of the Week" on the whiteboard before your first class of the week.
2. Start the lesson by telling the class, "The Word of the Week is _____."
3. Ask the class, "Who can tell me what this word

means? It's okay to tell me in your own words."
Respond to their answers positively, even if they're
totally off-base; remember, they're kids and the
youngest of them can only relate to their own
experiences.

4. Speak aloud and write the "formal definition" on
   the whiteboard.
5. Use an "opposite of" question to further clarify
   the concept for the class.
6. Provide a "let's pretend you..." example to help
   the children grasp the concept on the basis of a
   familiar experience.
7. Close with a simplified review of the day's lesson
   and positive feedback on how well they listened,
   etc.

OTHER IMPORTANT CONSIDERATIONS

Maintaining order during mat chat time is essential to
meeting learning objectives in the allotted time frame.
Essentially, you only have ten minutes a week to instill a
lesson that drives home the importance of each Word of the
Week. That means a single disruptive student can throw the
whole lesson off, and prevent the rest of the class from
getting the lesson.

This also means that structure is even more important
during mat chats. Here are a few things you can do to ensure
that you keep the lesson structured and disciplined, while
still keeping your students engaged:

Posture: All your kids should know their "listening and learning position". This means they sit "legs crossed, shoulders back, head up, and hands on your knees." You can cue this position by anchoring it to a phrase, like "Black Belt Focus!" Over time, your students will know when you say, "Black Belt Focus!" that they need to sit up straight and listen.

Positive Reinforcement: Let kids know when they're doing well, always. When the class sits down, pick a child out that is really sitting up and showing "Black Belt Focus" and highlight them by telling everyone how good they're doing and how proud you are of them. Shortly, you'll see the rest of the class following suit. Tell them all how great they're doing.

Avoid Giving False Praise: Just make sure you avoid giving praise for the sake of praise. If you fall into this trap, you'll soon find that the kids in your classes have figured out you're giving false praise, and your praise will become ineffective and meaningless. So, look for what they're doing correctly and praise them for it, but also remember that it's okay to correct them as well.

Keep The Lesson On Track: There's always going to be that kid that just rambles on; your job is to keep the lesson on track while still making your students feel like rock stars. So, remind the class to keep their answers short, and be ready to interject with a compliment to keep things moving whenever a kid gets long-winded and starts to ramble or take the conversation off-topic.

Use The Wiggles: You're always going to have that kid that can't sit still. So, use this to your advantage. When you see a child who is losing focus, call on them with a smile and compliment their response. They'll know they got "caught," but they'll also respond well to the fact that you're helping them focus with positive reinforcement.

Have a Fun Drill Handy: Having a fun drill ready to go after your mat chat is a fantastic way to motivate your class to listen and engage. If they know that they have to behave and listen in order to participate in the game you have planned at the end of class, believe me they'll do exactly that.

Do Not Allow Parents to Disrupt Your Class: Be polite, but let parents know that speaking to their children during class is an absolute no-no. I tell my kids and parents both that from the time we bow-in to the time we bow-out, they should pretend that they don't see each other. This can actually be a fun game for some kids; encourage your parents to reward their children after class with positive verbal reinforcement when they focus all the way through class.

Using a Student Creed

Having a student creed that your class recites both before and at the end of class is a powerful way to reinforce your character development lessons. The following is a student creed I learned from Greg Silva of United Professionals that I adopted for use in my own schools.

Student Creed

1. I will develop myself in a positive manner, and avoid that which could reduce my mental growth or physical health.
2. I will develop self-discipline in order to bring out the best in myself and others.

3. I will use common sense before self-defense, and never be abusive to myself or others.

It's a simple thing to implement, but using such a student creed and having students recite it at the beginning and end of class can have a profound impact on their attitudes. Plus, it allows those parents who only come inside when they have to get their kids to see what you're teaching. Use it and you'll soon see what I mean.

Word Power Phrases

The use of "word power phrases" is a concept I learned from Zulfi Ahmed of Bushi-Ban International. Word power commands and responses are used in the classroom environment to instill self-esteem and unity in your students. They're essentially verbal command-response patterns that you can use during your classes to help further reinforce the character development lessons you're teaching during your mat chats.

When I started using them in my classes, I noticed an immediate improvement in my students' focus, posture, and enthusiasm for learning. I also received a lot of positive feedback from parents as well (again, this is directly related to providing opportunities for parents to observe what their children are learning in your classes).

If you're going to use them, I suggest that you require all students to have the phrases memorized before they receive their first belt. Here are the phrases I adapted for use in my own classes; feel free to modify their use in your own classes.

Command/Response (You say/they respond)

"Attention" / "I'm a winner, sir!"

"Bow"/ "Future black belt, sir!"

"Ready position" / "We are champions, sir!"

"Fighting stance!" / "To defend with honor and pride, sir!"

"Eyes on who?"/ "You, sir!"

"3 rules of concentration!" / "Focus with the eyes, focus with the mind, focus with the body, sir!"

4

THE CHARACTER DEVELOPMENT
LESSON PLANS

A 16-WEEK CURRICULUM WITH 32 LESSONS BASED ON
TRADITIONAL MARTIAL ARTS VALUES

I n this book, we'll be focusing on teaching the following terms as key values that comprise the central component of our martial arts philosophy, and in turn our character values curriculum. I personally believe that teaching the ideals of self-improvement and self-excellence, responsibility in our actions, and being kind to others is essential for helping our children live healthy, productive lives.

I've chosen the following character values for both their universally admired status across many cultures and religions, as well as for their value when taught in the context of life skills lessons to children. I've referred to the standard dictionary entry for the abbreviated definition that immediately follows each term; however, the lessons themselves are based on my life experiences, my Judeo-Christian belief system, and the time I spent studying ethics and leadership at the graduate level in university.

I believe you'll find these lessons to have universal application, no matter your personal background or beliefs. Remember, in the end it's your school and your curriculum, so it's up to you how much or how little you adapt these lessons to suit your own personal and moral philosophy. Just be aware that these lessons have been proven over the last twenty years to have a universal appeal and impact among families from all backgrounds and belief systems, and you will likely get the best results by teaching the lessons exactly as they are outlined in this book.

- **Courtesy** - "formal politeness"; to be shown to others at all times
- **Growth** - "to flourish"; always keep learning and improving
- **Courage** - "valor"; not the absence of fear, but going on in spite of fear
- **Sincerity** - "being genuine"; mean what you say and do what you mean
- **Honesty** - "being truthful"; always seek to do what is right
- **Obedience** - "a sense of duty"; fulfilling obligations and following the rules
- **Humility** - "freedom from pride"; avoid becoming foolishly over-confident
- **Perseverance** - "to persist"; have a "never give up" attitude
- **Honor** - "a sense of right and truth"; know right from wrong and do right
- **Loyalty** - "faithfulness"; being true to others and what is right

- **Self-control** - "handling your actions properly"; choosing the right actions at all times
- **Knowledge** - "that which is known"; applied knowledge is power
- **Respect** - "esteem"; give it to others, earn it for yourself
- **Integrity** - "soundness of character"; living by right beliefs

Over the following pages, I'll be introducing each of these character values in two individual weekly lesson plans to be taught at the end of your child-age classes. Each lesson is split up into two different lessons; one for the first half of the week, and one for the second half. You can feel free to teach it all in one class; however, I find that reinforcement helps to make these lessons stick over the long-term.

How Often Should You Teach These Lessons?

I prefer to rotate the lessons over a 16 week period with my own personal child safety curriculum, which I also designed to be taught in 16 weeks. That way, children are repeating each lesson approximately every eight months, which is not so often as to bore them, but not so far apart that they forget each lesson's meaning over time.

5

WEEK ONE
COURTESY

C ourtesy - "formal politeness"; to be shown to others at all times.

Week 1, Lesson 1

1. Write "Courtesy" on the whiteboard before your first class of the week.
2. Start the lesson by telling the class, "Class, the Word of the Week is Courtesy."
3. Ask the class, "Who can tell me what this word means? It's okay to tell me in your own words." Remember to respond to their answers positively, even if they're totally off-base; remember, they're kids and the youngest can only relate to their own experiences.
4. Say, "The dictionary says courtesy is formal

politeness," and write "formal politeness" on the whiteboard. Explain what "formal" means by using the example of bowing when you start and finish class, and using "the seven courtesy words": *yes sir, no sir, yes ma'am, no ma'am, thank you, you're welcome, and please.*

5. Use an "opposite of" question to further clarify the concept for the class: "So, is courtesy being mean and rude? Of course not. Instead, *courtesy is treating other people the way you want to be treated.*" (You may want to repeat that last part again.) "So, if you want people to be nice to you, you should first be nice to them."

6. Provide a "let's pretend you..." example to help the children grasp the concept on the basis of a familiar experience: "Class, let's pretend you're out on the playground with your friend waiting your turn to go on the slide, and another kid comes over and just cuts in line in front of you. Is that using courtesy? No, of course not - that would be rude! Now, let's say someone gave you a present, and you said 'thank you!' - is that using courtesy? Yes, it is! It's polite to say thank you when someone gives you a gift or when they do something nice for you. And, thank you is one of our "seven courtesy words."

7. Close with a simplified review of the day's lesson and positive feedback on how well they listened, etc.

WEEK 1, Lesson 2

1. Start with a review of the lesson from earlier in the week. Review what courtesy is (treating other the way you want to be treated).

2. Ask the class, "Now, who can tell me one of the seven courtesy words?" Keep calling on kids until you've written all seven on the board. Compliment them each on answering correctly, even if they provide repeats.

3. Now, go through each courtesy word and ask for an example of when to use it. Be ready to help them out by providing hints and clues. For example: "Okay, so when would we use 'yes sir' or 'yes ma'am'? That's right, like when a parent or a teacher asks you a question."

4. Give the class an assignment to start using their courtesy words with their parents for practice at home. Parents will love you for this; just remember that you have to reinforce it by reminding kids every week to use their courtesy words with their parents.

5. Close with a simplified review of the week's lessons and provide positive feedback on how well they listened, etc.

6

WEEK TWO
GROWTH

G rowth - "to flourish"; always keep learning and improving

WEEK 2, Lesson 1

1. Write "Growth" on the whiteboard before your first class of the week.
2. Start the lesson by telling the class, "Class, the Word of the Week is Growth."
3. Ask the class, "Who can tell me what this word means? It's okay to tell me in your own words." Remember to respond to their answers positively, even if they're totally off-base; remember, they're kids and the youngest can only relate to their own experiences.

4. Say, "The dictionary says growth means to flourish," and write "to flourish" on the whiteboard. Explain what "flourish" means by saying it means something is growing up big and strong.

5. This week we need to take a different tact for teaching this Word of the Week. Instead of using an "opposite" example, we need to jump right in by asking a question. Ask the class, "So, growth means getting bigger and stronger, right?"

6. Now we're going to explain the three ways we can grow. "Class, there are three ways we can grow. We can grow in the body, in the mind, and in the heart. Somebody tell me what they think it means to grow in the body. *(Pick someone at random.)* That's right! It means getting bigger and stronger. How can we help our bodies become bigger and stronger? Yes! By eating good healthy food. What's another way? Yes! Exercise. And, what's another way? *(Most classes won't get this one.)* That's right, by getting plenty of sleep! These are the three ways we can help our bodies grow bigger and stronger. Also, we need to make sure we don't do anything harmful to our body, like eating too much junk food, or smoking, or drinking alcohol, or taking illegal drugs." *(That last part may be a little much for your youngest students, so you might leave it out in your tots class.)*

7. Close with a simplified review of the day's lesson

and positive feedback on how well they listened, etc.

WEEK 2, Lesson 2

1. Start with a review of the lesson from earlier in the week. Review what the three ways are that we can grow (in the body, mind, and heart).

2. Ask the class, "Now, who can tell me what you think it means to grow in the mind? That's right! It means to learn more in school. That means we have to pay attention in school, study hard, and do our best to get excellent grades. We have a saying in martial arts, 'Knowledge is power!' What do you think that means? Very good! Knowledge lets you do the things you want to do. For example, knowledge can allow you to get a good job, write a book, become a doctor or an astronaut... pretty much anything you want to do, you can do it if you'll only spend the time to learn how and study hard."

3. Next part of the lesson is on growing in the heart. "Okay, who can tell me what they think it means to grow in the heart? Very good! It means becoming a better person. That means we try our best to be nice to other people, each and every day. Why is that important? Yes, it goes back to what we learned last week - courtesy. If we want

other people to be nice to us, we need to treat
them exactly the way we want to be treated."

4. Close with a simplified review of the week's
   lessons and provide positive feedback on how
   well they listened, etc.

7

WEEK THREE
COURAGE

C ourage - "valor"; not the absence of fear, but going on in spite of fear

Week 3, Lesson 1

1. Write "Courage" on the whiteboard before your first class of the week.
2. Start the lesson by telling the class, "Class, the Word of the Week is Courage."
3. Ask the class, "Who can tell me what this word means? It's okay to tell me in your own words." Remember to respond to their answers positively, even if they're totally off-base; remember, they're kids and the youngest can only relate to their own experiences.
4. Say, "The dictionary says courage means 'valor',"

and write "valor" on the whiteboard. Explain what "valor" means by saying it means being very brave.

5. This week we need to take a different tact for teaching the Word of the Week. Instead of using an "opposite" example, we need to jump right in by asking a question. Ask the class, "So, does courage mean you're not afraid of anything?" *(Most kids will say that being brave means you aren't afraid of anything, which is obviously not true.)*

6. Now we're going to explain why having real courage means you do brave things, even if you're afraid. "Now hang on... isn't everyone afraid of something? Sure they are! That's just part of being a regular person. Now, what people can we name that are very brave? *(Kids at this point might give examples of firefighters, police, soldiers, etc.)* Yes, those are all very brave people. But, do you think a firefighter isn't afraid of going into a burning building to save people? Sure they are. But they do it anyway, because it's important. They have to save those people because it's their job, and people are depending on them. So, they do it, everyday, even when they're afraid. That's courage."

7. Close with a simplified review of the day's lesson and provide positive feedback on how well they listened, etc.

WEEK 3, Lesson 2

1. Start with a review of the lesson from earlier in the week. Review what it means to have courage (doing things that need to be done, even if you're afraid).

2. Ask the class, "What kind of things might scare you that are important to do? *(Field a few questions and then move on.)* What if you had to give a report in front of your class, but you were afraid that people would laugh at you. Still, you have to do it, right? So, getting up there and speaking in front of your class is real courage, because you're doing something that's important to do, even if it makes you afraid."

3. The next part of the lesson is about how things we're afraid of often aren't that scary after we do them. "Sometimes, the things we're scared of aren't so scary after we do them. Things like riding a bike for the first time without training wheels, or riding a roller coaster, sleeping with the night light off, or giving a report in front of our class at school. That's another good reason for having courage, so we can overcome our fears."

4. Next, we need to talk about the difference between being brave and being foolish. "Now, what if someone dares us to do something dangerous and they call us chicken because we won't do it. Does that mean we don't have courage? Of course not! If someone dares you to

jump off the roof of your house, that's being foolish - you'd get hurt! That person is the *real* chicken, because they're trying to trick you into doing something dangerous. So remember, courage is only about doing important things, like when a firefighter saves people. Courage is not about taking foolish dares that get people hurt."

5. Close with a simplified review of the week's lessons and provide positive feedback on how well they listened, etc.

8

WEEK FOUR
SINCERITY

S incerity - "being genuine"; mean what you say and do what you mean

WEEK 4, Lesson 1

1. Write "Sincerity" on the whiteboard before your first class of the week.
2. Start the lesson by telling the class, "Class, the Word of the Week is Sincerity."
3. Ask the class, "Who can tell me what this word means? It's okay to tell me in your own words." Respond to their answers in a positive manner, even if they're totally off-base; remember, they're kids and the youngest can only relate to their own experiences.
4. Say, "The dictionary says sincerity means 'being

genuine',", and write "being genuine" on the whiteboard. Explain what "genuine" means by saying it means being for real and not being fake.

5. This week we're going to start the lesson by asking the class if they've ever had someone act like they were their friend, when they really weren't. Ask the class, "Have you ever had someone give you a compliment, but later you found out that they really didn't mean it? Maybe they did it just because you had something they wanted, like candy or a game that they wanted to play, or a toy they wanted to play with. How did that make you feel?" *(Try to field their answers as a group.)* "It made you feel bad, right? Why?" *(You'll get a variety of answers for this, but basically you want to focus on how people who act nice when they really aren't are living a lie.)* "Right - it's because you were being lied to, and that's not nice."

6. Now we're going to explain what our definition of sincerity is: "So sincerity is meaning what you say. That means you tell the truth! Also, it can mean that if you can't say anything nice, don't say anything at all. If you're really being sincere, then you aren't going to say something you don't mean just to get on someone's good side. But that also means we have to know when it's best to just not say anything - because we have to respect other people's feelings too."

7. Close with a simplified review of the day's lesson

and provide positive feedback on how well they listened, etc.

WEEK 4, Lesson 2

1. Start with a review of the lesson from earlier in the week. Review what it means to be sincere (saying what you mean, and meaning what you do).

2. Now it's time to talk about being sincere in how we act. "We already talked about being sincere with our words. Now, let's talk about the second half of being sincere, which is acting sincere. Have you ever had someone act like they liked you, when they really didn't? How did that make you feel? It made you feel bad, right? That's because it is just as hurtful to act like you like someone just because you want something from them, as it is to lie to them. It is the same thing. So, we have to be sincere in what we say, and also in what we do. Just remember, sincerity isn't an excuse to be mean to people if we don't like them. We still have to be courteous. But, it does mean that we shouldn't be nice to people just to get what we want from them. That is mean and it is called taking advantage."

3. Ask the class, "So we know it's important to mean what we say, and not be fake by pretending we

like someone just to get things we want. But why is that so important?" *(This is a very abstract concept, so pause for a moment and then continue.)* "It's because we want to be trustworthy - that means we want to be the type of person that people can trust. Remember the story of the boy who cried wolf? He pretended that a big bad wolf was coming just to scare people, because he thought it was funny. What happened when the wolf really came? That's right, no one believed him because they all knew he was a big faker. So, be sincere in your words and your actions, and you'll soon become the type of person people will trust."

4. Close with a simplified review of the week's lessons and provide positive feedback on how well they listened, etc.

9

WEEK FIVE
HONESTY

Honesty - "being truthful"; always seek to do what is right

WEEK 5, Lesson 1

1. Write "Honesty" on the whiteboard before your first class of the week.
2. Start the lesson by telling the class, "Class, the Word of the Week is Honesty."
3. Ask the class, "Who can tell me what this word means? It's okay to tell me in your own words." Respond to their answers in a positive manner, even if they're totally off-base; remember, they're kids and the youngest can only relate to their own experiences.
4. Say, "The dictionary says honesty means 'being

truthful','" and write "being truthful" on the whiteboard. Explain what "honesty" means by saying it means that you always speak the truth and always try to do what it right.

5. This week we're going to start the lesson by asking the class if they've ever had someone lie to them. Ask the class, "Have you ever had someone lie to you? How did that make you feel?" *(Try to field their answers as a group.)* "It made you feel bad, right? Why?" *(You'll get a variety of answers for this, but basically you want to focus on how lying is morally wrong because it is a betrayal of trust.)* "Right - it's because you felt like you were being tricked, and you trusted that person to tell you the truth. When they lied to you, it hurt your feelings."

6. Now we need to go a little deeper to clarify just why lying is wrong. "So, the reason lying is wrong is because it is hurtful to trick people who trust you. When someone trusts you, you have to respect their feelings. Lying to them isn't being trustworthy. Don't you want to be someone people can trust? Of course you do! And, guess what? Other people will come to admire you and look up to you if you are the type of person they can trust."

7. Close with a simplified review of the day's lesson and provide positive feedback on how well they listened, etc.

Week 5, Lesson 2

1. Start with a review of the lesson from earlier in the week. Review what it means to be honest (being truthful in what we say and always seeking to do what's right).

2. Now it's time to talk about being honest in our actions. "We already talked about being honest in what we say. Now, let's talk about the second half of being honest, which is being honest in our actions. Let's pretend that you worked really hard to save up your allowance so you could buy a new bike. After months of saving, you finally had saved enough, so your parents took you to the store and you picked out exactly the bike you wanted. But, you accidentally left it outside overnight and someone stole it. How would that make you feel? Right, it would make you very upset! That was your bike, and if someone took it from you it would be wrong, because that is stealing. Stealing is probably the most common *dishonest* thing people do." Explain how "dishonest" means not being honest.

3. Tell the class, "So, honesty is also important because it is a way that we respect the rights and property of others. If we lived in a world where people just took things from other people whenever they wanted, we'd all be fighting and

stealing all the time. And, that wouldn't be a very nice place to live. That's why it's important to be honest, so we can live in a world where people can trust one another and respect one another, and be respected back as well."

4. Close with a simplified review of the week's lessons and provide positive feedback on how well they listened, etc.

10

WEEK SIX

OBEDIENCE

O bedience - "a sense of duty"; fulfilling obligations and following the rules

Week 6, Lesson 1

1. Write "Obedience" on the whiteboard before your first class of the week.
2. Start the lesson by telling the class, "Class, the Word of the Week is Obedience."
3. Ask the class, "Who can tell me what this word means? It's okay to tell me in your own words." Respond to their answers in a positive manner, even if they're totally off-base; remember, they're kids and the youngest can only relate to their own experiences.
4. Say, "The dictionary says obedience means 'a

sense of duty',", and write it on the whiteboard. Explain what "obedience" means by saying it means that you take care of your obligations to others and follow the rules.

5. This week we're going to start the lesson by explaining what an *obligation* is; ask the class, "Does anyone know what an obligation is?" Don't be surprised if you get a bunch of blank stares, because again, this is an abstract concept. So, we need to explain it in terms they can understand. "Okay, let's say you get an allowance for doing chores around the house. That means you have an obligation to do your chores, and your parents also have an obligation to pay you your allowance when you do your chores."

6. Now we need to go a little deeper to explain what happens when people ignore their obligations. "So, let's pretend that you decided you didn't want to do your chores this week because you wanted to play video games instead. What would happen? That's right, the trash would pile up in the kitchen, the dishes would pile up in the sink, and of course, you wouldn't get your allowance at the end of the week. So, when we don't live up to our obligations, bad things can happen. But what happens when we take care of our obligations? That's right; we get rewarded for our work. Sometimes that may just mean that we receive a compliment or good grades. But, as we get older those good grades can turn into a good job and

having the freedom to do what we want with our lives. So, taking care of our obligations is how we learn to have responsibility, and although it's not always fun, responsibility helps us have happier lives."

7. Close with a simplified review of the day's lesson and provide positive feedback on how well they listened, etc.

WEEK 6, Lesson 2

1. Start with a review of the lesson from earlier in the week. Review what it means to be obedient (taking care of your obligations to others and following the rules).

2. Now it's time to talk about following rules. "We already talked last week about how we are rewarded for taking care of our obligations. That's one side of being obedient. Now, there's another side to being obedient, and that is following the rules. Do you have rules in your house that you have to follow? Who wants to share a rule that they have at home?" Call on several children and allow them to share their home rules.

3. Tell the class, "Yes, and there's a very good reason we have rules like no running in the house, bed time is at 8 PM on school nights, and always eat your vegetables. The reason is because those rules

help us to be healthy and happy and safe. See, your parents love you and they know what is best for you, and that's why they have rules. Even though sometimes the rules your parents have for you may not seem fair, remember that your parents love you and they want the best for you. So, sometimes they have to make rules that aren't fun so you'll be healthy and safe. Now, can you see why it's important to be obedient? That's right, so we can be healthy, happy, and safe."

4. Close with a simplified review of the week's lessons and provide positive feedback on how well they listened, etc.

11

WEEK SEVEN
HUMILITY

Humility - "freedom from pride"; avoid becoming foolishly over-confident

WEEK 7, Lesson 1

1. Write "Humility" on the whiteboard before your first class of the week.
2. Start the lesson by telling the class, "Class, the Word of the Week is Humility."
3. Ask the class, "Who can tell me what this word means? It's okay to tell me in your own words." Respond to their answers in a positive manner, even if they're totally off-base; remember, they're kids and the youngest can only relate to their own experiences.
4. Say, "The dictionary says humility means

'freedom from pride',", and write it on the whiteboard. Explain what "humility" means by saying it means to avoid becoming foolishly over-confident.

5. Now we need to explain the difference between confidence and cockiness. "Okay, so we all know that it's good to be confident, because we have to believe that we can be successful in whatever we set out to do. But, there's a difference between being confident and being arrogant and prideful. Confidence is good because it means we believe we can succeed; arrogance is bad because when someone is arrogant it means they think they're better than everyone else. Have you ever known someone like that? Those people can be really hard to be around."

6. Now we need to go a little deeper to explain why humility is a virtue. "When someone has humility we say they are humble. Being humble isn't about being weak. It's about believing in your ability to succeed, while still being smart enough to know that you don't know everything, and that you need the help of others to achieve success in life. Also, it means that we treat others as equals, no matter how much money they have, what kind of clothes they wear, or what neighborhood they come from. Humility has a lot to do with courtesy, because when you treat other people as equals you are treating them with respect."

7. Close with a simplified review of the day's lesson

and provide positive feedback on how well they listened, etc.

Week 7, Lesson 2

1. Start with a review of the lesson from earlier in the week. Review what it means to have humility (to avoid becoming foolishly over-confident).

2. Now it's time to talk about being humble in the martial arts or other things we are good at doing. "In the martial arts we have a saying that there's always someone tougher than you are. I think that goes for just about anything we can do, whether it's being good at martial arts, or other sports, or school, or music, or dance, or whatever. There is always going to be someone better than you so it's good to remember that there is always going to be someone you can learn from. Remember that every sensei has a sensei, and every black belt learned from another black belt who knew more than they did. Every teacher has a teacher, and it's only by being humble that we can become good students so that knowledge is passed on from teacher to student."

3. Now it's time to relate this to something practical. Tell the class, "That goes for school as well. Your teachers became teachers by going to school for a long time. Sometimes, you might be tempted to

think that you're smarter than they are, but you should always remember that they have been in school a lot longer than you have. Also, we need to remember that being humble is about being respectful to our elders. Remember how we talked about treating others as equals? Well, we also need to show special respect for people like our parents and teachers as well. That's as much a part of humility as anything we've learned this week."

4. Close with a simplified review of the week's lessons and provide positive feedback on how well they listened, etc.

12

WEEK EIGHT
PERSEVERANCE

P erseverance - "to persist"; have a "never give up" attitude

WEEK 8, Lesson 1

1. Write "Perseverance" on the whiteboard before your first class of the week.
2. Start the lesson by telling the class, "Class, the Word of the Week is Perseverance."
3. Ask the class, "Who can tell me what this word means? It's okay to tell me in your own words." Respond to their answers in a positive manner, even if they're totally off-base; remember, they're kids and the youngest can only relate to their own experiences.
4. Say, "The dictionary says Perseverance means 'to

persist'," and write it on the whiteboard. Explain what "Perseverance" means by saying it means to never give up.

5. Now we need to talk about the importance of Perseverance. "Have you ever tried to learn or do something that was really hard and frustrating? I know I have." *(Relate a personal story where you struggled to overcome a personal challenge. It will help your students immensely if they can know that you sometimes struggle just like they do.)* "But, because I never gave up I was able to achieve my goal."

6. Now we need to go a little deeper to help our class understand how to develop the attitude to persevere in the face of hardship. "Who here knows who Albert Einstein was? That's right; he was one of the greatest scientists we've ever known. But, did you know that Albert Einstein didn't speak until he was four years old, and he didn't learn to read until he was seven? He was even expelled from school for being a daydreamer and his teachers thought he would never amount to anything! Yet, he believed in his ability to learn and become great, and I think that's an important lesson for all of us. There's a really great saying that I like about perseverance that I think Einstein knew, and it goes like this; 'If I believe it, then I can achieve it.' I want you to repeat that to yourself, anytime you are facing a tough challenge and you want to quit. Just keep telling yourself, 'If I believe it, I can achieve it.'"

7. Close with a simplified review of the day's lesson and provide positive feedback on how well they listened, etc.

Week 8, Lesson 2

1. Start with a review of the lesson from earlier in the week. Review what it means to have perseverance (to never give up).

2. Now it's time to talk about quitting too soon. "You know, there's another saying that I like, and I'm sure you've heard this before. 'Quitters never win, and winners never quit.' I bet you've heard that before from a teacher, a coach, or your parents. But it's funny how we hear things and never really think about what they mean. Who can tell me what that means?"

3. Now it's time to put this in practical terms. Tell the class, "Here's the thing about people who quit and people who succeed. When you talk to successful people, they'll tell you that the only difference between them and others who failed is that they didn't give up. Now, think about the light bulb. Thomas Edison was a famous inventor, and he invented the modern light bulb. But did you know that he failed 1,000 times before he successfully created a light bulb that would last? When he was asked how it felt to fail 1,000 times, he said, 'I

didn't fail 1,000 times. The light bulb was an invention with 1,000 steps.' And that's the attitude you have to have if you want to succeed."

4. Close with a simplified review of the week's lessons and provide positive feedback on how well they listened, etc.

13

WEEK NINE
HONOR

H onor - "a sense of right and truth"; knowing right from wrong and doing what is right

WEEK 9, Lesson 1

1. Write "Honor" on the whiteboard before your first class of the week.
2. Start the lesson by telling the class, "Class, the Word of the Week is Honor."
3. Ask the class, "Who can tell me what this word means? It's okay to tell me in your own words." Respond to their answers in a positive manner, even if they're totally off-base; remember, they're kids and the youngest can only relate to their own experiences.
4. Say, "The dictionary says Honor means 'a sense of

right and truth'," and write it on the whiteboard. Explain what "honor" means by saying it means knowing right from wrong and doing what is right.

5. Now we need to introduce the first concept, knowing right from wrong. "So, how do we know right from wrong... where do we learn that? That's right, we learn right from wrong from our parents. From the time you were old enough to talk, your parents have been teaching you right from wrong. We also learn right from wrong from our grandparents, aunts and uncles, older brothers and sisters, teachers, and at church or synagogue. But the final say about right and wrong for you is from your parents."

6. Now it's time to discuss the need for right and wrong. "Some people say that right and wrong is different for everyone. But that's a lot like saying that colors look different to everyone. Even though you can't explain why red is red and blue is blue, you know what blue and red look like. Knowing right from wrong is a lot like that, because somewhere deep inside you just know the difference between right and wrong. Right and wrong comes from having respect for other people, for the rights and property of others, for their feelings, and from wanting the world to be a good and decent place to live in. If no one ever did what was right, and they only did what felt good to them at the time, the world would be a very bad

place. Living honorably - that means living with honor - is knowing right from wrong, and always doing what you know is right because you want the world to be a better place."

7. Close with a simplified review of the day's lesson and provide positive feedback on how well they listened, etc.

WEEK 9, Lesson 2

1. Start with a review of the lesson from earlier in the week. Review what it means to live honorably (knowing right from wrong and doing what is right).

2. Now it's time to talk about how to know right from wrong when there isn't an adult around to ask. "So how do we figure out right from wrong when our parents aren't around? For starters, you should always go back to what they've taught you. And, we can pretty much figure out right from wrong by asking ourselves four questions: 'Is this something that will hurt someone? Is this something that will hurt me? Is this something that I would want done to me? What would my parents think about this?' Those four questions will help you to know right from wrong, even when your mom or dad isn't there to tell you what to do."

3. Now it's time to put this in practical terms. Tell the class, "Remember that when you choose to do what is right, you are choosing to live honorably. That is part of what it means to be a warrior and not just a martial artist. A warrior chooses to live with honor, and to live for something more than just his or her own needs. Instead of just living selfishly, a warrior thinks about how their actions will affect others, and chooses to live a life that serves the needs of others as well as their own. That, I think, is a very honorable way to live."

4. Close with a simplified review of the week's lessons and provide positive feedback on how well they listened, etc.

14

WEEK TEN
LOYALTY

L oyalty - "faithfulness"; being true to others and what is right

WEEK 10, Lesson 1

1. Write "Loyalty" on the whiteboard before your first class of the week.
2. Start the lesson by telling the class, "Class, the Word of the Week is Loyalty."
3. Ask the class, "Who can tell me what this word means? It's okay to tell me in your own words." Respond to their answers in a positive manner, even if they're totally off-base; remember, they're kids and the youngest can only relate to their own experiences.
4. Say, "The dictionary says loyalty means

'faithfulness'," and write it on the whiteboard.
Explain what "faithfulness" means by saying it
means being true to others and being true to what
is right.

5. Now we need to introduce the first concept, being
   true to others. "Does anyone know what it means
   to be faithful? Have you ever heard someone say
   that they had a 'faithful friend'? What kind of
   friend is that? That's right - a friend forever.
   Someone who will stick by you through thick and
   thin. Dogs are like that, they're very faithful pets,
   and very loyal to their owners. That's why people
   say that dogs are faithful, because they make very
   good friends."

6. Now it's time to apply this in practical terms.
   "Have you ever had a friend that stopped being
   your friend for some reason? Maybe you got into
   an argument and they stopped being your friend.
   Or, maybe they started hanging out with kids that
   are more popular instead of you. Is that a very
   good friend? Of course not, because a good friend,
   a true friend, is a friend that is loyal to the end.
   That's the kind of friend you want to have, and
   that's the sort of friend you should be."

7. Close with a simplified review of the day's lesson
   and provide positive feedback on how well they
   listened, etc.

WEEK 10, Lesson 2

1. Start with a review of the lesson from earlier in the week. Review what it means to be loyal (being true and faithful to others and being true and faithful to what is right).

2. Now it's time to talk about being true and faithful to what is right. "Okay, we all know that it's important to be faithful to others. And we especially need to be faithful to our family, and faithful to our friends. But can we be faithful to ideas as well as people? Sure we can."

3. Now it's time to put this in practical terms. Tell the class, "For starters, we need to be faithful to our beliefs. Of course, first we have to believe in something that's worth believing in. For example, I believe in *(God, being loyal to my country, being nice to others, helping other people, always doing what it right, etc.)*. That belief is important to me, because it is part of what makes me who I am. Now, what kind of person would I be if I was only loyal to my beliefs when it was easy or convenient? Not very loyal, right?"

4. Now it's time to take it a little further. "Some people are willing to forget or change their beliefs so they can fit in, or to make people like them who don't share the same beliefs. But, the problem with doing that is people won't respect you if you change your beliefs just to fit in. My advice to you is that you figure out what you believe in based on

what is good and true and that you stick by those beliefs even when it makes you unpopular or disliked. Because, loyalty is about more than being true to others, it's also about being loyal to beliefs that help us to be better people."

5. Close with a simplified review of the week's lessons and provide positive feedback on how well they listened, etc.

15

WEEK ELEVEN
SELF-CONTROL

S elf-Control - "handling your actions properly"; choosing the right actions at all times

WEEK 11, Lesson 1

1. Write "Self-Control" on the whiteboard before your first class of the week.
2. Start the lesson by telling the class, "Class, the Word of the Week is Self-Control."
3. Ask the class, "Who can tell me what this word means? It's okay to tell me in your own words." Respond to their answers in a positive manner, even if they're totally off-base; remember, they're kids and the youngest can only relate to their own experiences.
4. Say, "The dictionary says self-control means

'handling your actions properly','" and write it on the whiteboard. Explain what that means by saying it means choosing the right thing to do and doing it, even when you don't want to.

5. Now we need to go a little deeper to help them understand. "Have you ever been so mad that you wanted to break something? I think we've all been so angry we wanted to scream, right? The thing is, everyone gets angry. But, what kind of world would it be if everyone acted out on their anger, all the time? That's right, it'd make the world a pretty scary place if people were screaming and yelling and fighting all the time."

6. Now it's time to apply this in practical terms. "So, we have to remember that self-control - meaning controlling how we act - is really important. We have to have self-control, because no one wants to live in a world where everyone is fighting, yelling, and arguing all the time. So, here's what I want you to do the next time you get so angry you want to scream. Stop, close your eyes, and count to ten in your head while you take some deep breaths. Let each breath be a number. Breathe in and out; that's one. Breathe in and out again; that's two. By the time you get to ten, I'll bet you're able to think more clearly and that you're not nearly as upset."

7. Close with a simplified review of the day's lesson and provide positive feedback on how well they listened, etc.

Week 11, Lesson 2

1. Start with a review of the lesson from earlier in the week. Review what it means to have self-control (choosing the right thing to do and doing it, even when you don't want to).

2. Now it's time to talk about the benefits of self-control. "Okay, so we know that having self-control makes the world a better place. That's great, but let's talk today about what self-control does for you. Have you ever known someone who had poor self-control? Maybe they yelled a lot, or they were always talking in class during quiet time, or they were really angry all the time and they hit people. Did you want to be around that person? Of course not, because no one wants to be around someone who yells a lot, who hits people, or who gets other people in trouble."

3. Now it's time to put this in personal terms. Tell the class, "So, we need to have self-control because it helps us get along well with others. If you want to have a lot of friends, and be admired and respected by others, learn to be a person with a lot of self-control. When someone yells at you, stay calm. When you get angry, breathe and count to ten. When things don't go your way, instead of stomping your feet and throwing a fit, relax and show the world that you can handle it. That's

having self-control, and it shows people that you are someone who is mature and who can handle responsibility. It shows people that you are a leader."

4. Close with a simplified review of the week's lessons and provide positive feedback on how well they listened, etc.

16

WEEK TWELVE
KNOWLEDGE

K nowledge - "that which is known"; applied knowledge is power

WEEK 12, Lesson 1

1. Write "Knowledge" on the whiteboard before your first class of the week.
2. Start the lesson by telling the class, "Class, the Word of the Week is Knowledge."
3. Ask the class, "Who can tell me what this word means? It's okay to tell me in your own words." Respond to their answers in a positive manner, even if they're totally off-base; remember, they're kids and the youngest can only relate to their own experiences.
4. Say, "The dictionary says knowledge means 'that

which is known',", and write it on the whiteboard. Explain what that means by saying it means things that you learn.

5. We're going to start by explaining how we get knowledge, because that will help put it into context. "So, knowledge is what we know and learn. How do we get knowledge? That's right, in school, by reading books, and also by watching educational movies and shows. We can also gain knowledge by learning from other people, just like you do here in martial arts. You gain knowledge about martial arts from me."

6. Now it's time to talk about why knowledge is important. "What do we say about knowledge here at *(name of your school)*? That's right, we say 'knowledge is power'. And why is that? Yes, it's because knowledge helps us do great things. By gaining knowledge in school, we can get good grades, which will lead to going to college or trade school and learning how to get a good job. Maybe we want to build and race fast cars, or fly to the moon, or to compose music, or to be a heart surgeon, or to paint beautiful pictures. By gaining knowledge and learning from others, that's how we're able to do just that. By gaining knowledge, we also get the ability to choose the sort of life we want to live."

7. Close with a simplified review of the day's lesson and provide positive feedback on how well they listened, etc.

WEEK 12, Lesson 2

1. Start with a review of the lesson from earlier in the week. Review what knowledge is (knowledge is what we learn and know).

2. Now it's time to talk about the best way to become knowledgeable. "Okay, so we know that knowledge is important, and it's all about learning. And, we know where we get knowledge. But do you know what one of the best ways to get knowledge is? I'll tell you, it's learning to love to read. Maybe you don't like reading, or you're just not good at it, but let me tell you, reading is like riding a bike. It can be hard at first, but the more you do it, the easier it gets, and the more fun it can be."

3. Now it's time to put this in perspective. Tell the class, "Believe it or not, some people don't have the opportunity to learn how to read. Think about that. What if you had to go through life not being able to read a book, or even a street sign? What if you didn't know how to sign your name? That would make things very difficult, right? Some people never had the opportunity that you have - they were never able to go to school every day to learn how to read, and how to write, and to learn all the things that you learn in school."

4. "That's why we should really want to learn to

read. Because, even though it's easy to take it for granted, we need to realize how blessed we are to be able to go to school and learn. So, I want you to do your very best in school. Maybe school is something that comes easy for you, and maybe it doesn't. But, either way that's no reason to slack off and not do your very best. I want you to commit right now that you'll do your very best in school. Can you do that for me? Better yet, can you do that for yourself?"

5. Close with a simplified review of the week's lessons and provide positive feedback on how well they listened, etc.

17

WEEK THIRTEEN
RESPECT

R espect - "esteem"; give it to others, earn it for yourself

WEEK 13, Lesson 1

1. Write "Respect" on the whiteboard before your
   first class of the week.
2. Start the lesson by telling the class, "Class, the
   Word of the Week is Respect."
3. Ask the class, "Who can tell me what this word
   means? It's okay to tell me in your own words."
   Respond to their answers in a positive manner,
   even if they're totally off-base; remember, they're
   kids and the youngest can only relate to their own
   experiences.
4. Say, "The dictionary says respect is 'esteem'," and

write it on the whiteboard. Explain what 'esteem' means by saying it means treating people with extra-special courtesy. You might also talk about how 'self-esteem' means feeling good about yourself, and 'esteem for others' means you look up to them.

5. We're going to start by explaining who we give respect to, because that will help put it into context. "Okay, so respect is a special type of courtesy. It's not just courtesy, but extra-special courtesy. Who are we supposed to show respect to? That's right, to our parents. Who else? Yes, to teachers. Who else? Yes, to martial arts instructors. Who else? Yes, to adults in general. Very good!"

6. Now it's time to talk about why respect is important. "Remember how we talked about being humble? One of the things we discussed was being humble enough to learn from others. Also, remember when we talked about honor? One of things we talked about was obligations, right? Well, think about this; your parents spend most of their time and effort taking care of you, working so you can have a nice home to live in and food to eat, taking you to school so you can learn, paying for cool things like martial arts lessons... do you see where I'm going with this? So, don't you think they deserve some thanks for doing all those things for you? Of course they do. At your age you can't go get a job to pay them back

for all they do, and besides it would take you a lifetime to do it. Instead, the best way you can say thanks to your parents for all they do for you, is for you to show them respect. Believe me; they'll appreciate that more than all the money and gifts in the world. And the cool thing is you can do it every single day."

7. Close with a simplified review of the day's lesson and provide positive feedback on how well they listened, etc.

WEEK 13, Lesson 2

1. Start with a review of the lesson from earlier in the week. Review what respect is (an extra-special kind of courtesy).

2. Now it's time to talk about the best way to show respect. "Okay, so we know that respect is important, but what's the best and easiest way we can show respect to our parents?" *(Call on several children, you'll get a lot of good answers.)* "Okay, those are all good answers. But you know what the easiest way to show respect is? It's when we use our courtesy words. Let's review them: 'yes sir, no sir, yes ma'am, no ma'am, thank you, you're welcome, and please'. Great - you remembered them all! Now, I want you to remember to use

them when your parents speak to you. That's a great way to show respect."

3. Now it's time expand on this. Tell the class, "There are other ways to show respect too, like listening when an adult is talking, making eye contact when you are listening, sitting still and using Black Belt focus... I could go on and on. Can you name some other ways we can show respect to adults?"

4. "Those are all great answers! Now that we know how to show respect, I want you all to use what we've learned this week about respect at home and at school. Can you do that? Outstanding!"

5. Close with a simplified review of the week's lessons and provide positive feedback on how well they listened, etc.

18

WEEK FOURTEEN
INTEGRITY

I ntegrity - "soundness of character"; living by right beliefs

WEEK 14, Lesson 1

1. Write "Integrity" on the whiteboard before your first class of the week.
2. Start the lesson by telling the class, "Class, the Word of the Week is Integrity."
3. Ask the class, "Who can tell me what this word means? It's okay to tell me in your own words." Respond to their answers in a positive manner, even if they're totally off-base; remember, they're kids and the youngest can only relate to their own experiences.
4. Say, "The dictionary says integrity is 'soundness of

character', " and write it on the whiteboard. Explain what 'character' means by saying it means what type of person you are, whether you are a good person or a bad person, a trustworthy person or someone who cannot be trusted.

5. We're going to start by speaking more about integrity, because we need to put it into context. "Now, we've covered a lot of different Words of the Week so far. Integrity is the last one, and that's because it has to do with how well you are using everything you've learned about the other words of the week. If you have a lot of integrity, you are someone who is courteous, respectful, honest, and humble. A person with integrity is courageous, sincere, shows perseverance, is obedient, honorable, and has self-control. In other words, having integrity means that you are an all-around good person."

6. Now it's time to talk about why integrity is important. "Remember how when we spoke about honesty and sincerity we also talked about being trustworthy? There's an old saying, and I'm sure you've heard it, 'Actions speak louder than words.' What that means is that you can't always tell what kind of person someone is by what they say, but you can tell who they are by watching what they do. If a person has integrity, they do what they say they'll do. Someone who doesn't have integrity will say one thing, but they'll do another. Can you see how

having integrity makes you someone people can trust?"

7. Close with a simplified review of the day's lesson and provide positive feedback on how well they listened, etc.

Week 14, Lesson 2

1. Start with a review of the lesson from earlier in the week. Review what integrity is (living by right beliefs).

2. Now it's time to encourage a little self-examination. "Okay, so we know that we want to have integrity, because we want to be good people. Also, we want to try to be the type of person other people can respect and look up to. But the truth is that only you can make yourself a person of integrity. And, it's not what you do when everyone is watching, but what you do when no one is watching that makes you a person of integrity."

3. Now it's time expand on this. Tell the class, "Some people only do the right thing because they're afraid of getting caught. Those people are selfish, because they put their own needs in front of those of others. Other people do the right thing because they know it's right. That's much better, because those people know what is right, and they choose to do the right thing even if it isn't the best thing

for them personally. And, they do it even when no one is around to see. That's real integrity."

4. "So, I want you to spend some time this week thinking about your actions and whether you have been acting with integrity. This is difficult, because often we don't want to face up to our own faults. However, if you want to have real integrity, it starts with being honest with yourself about you own faults, so you can change your bad habits into good results."

5. Close with a simplified review of the week's lessons and provide positive feedback on how well they listened, etc.

19

WEEK FIFTEEN
REVIEW

R eview Weeks 1-7

WEEK 15, Lesson 1
Review the following:

1. **Courtesy** - "formal politeness"; to be shown to others at all times
2. **Growth** - "to flourish"; remain humble enough to always keep improving
3. **Courage** - "valor"; not the absence of fear, but going on in spite of fear
4. **Sincerity** - "being genuine"; mean what you say and do what you mean

QUESTIONS FOR REVIEW

Ask as you review each Word of the Week:

- Who can tell me what _____ is?
- Why is it important?
- How can we practice it in our daily lives?

WEEK 15, Lesson 2

Review the following:

1. **Honesty** - "being truthful"; always seek to do what is right
2. **Obedience** - "a sense of duty"; fulfilling obligations and following the rules
3. **Humility** - "freedom from pride"; avoid becoming foolishly over-confident

QUESTIONS FOR REVIEW

Ask as you review each Word of the Week:

- Who can tell me what _____ is?
- Why is it important?
- How can we practice it in our daily lives?

20

WEEK SIXTEEN
REVIEW

R eview Weeks 8-14

WEEK 16, Lesson 1
Review the following:

1. **Perseverance** - "to persist"; have a "never give up" attitude
2. **Honor** - "a sense of right and truth"; know right from wrong and do right
3. **Loyalty** - "faithfulness"; being true to others and what is right
4. **Self-control** - "handling your actions properly"; right action at all times

QUESTIONS FOR REVIEW

Ask as you review each Word of the Week:

- Who can tell me what _____ is?
- Why is it important?
- How can we practice it in our daily lives?

WEEK 16, Lesson 2

Review the following:

1. **Knowledge** - "that which is known"; applied knowledge is power
2. **Respect** - "esteem"; give it to others, earn it for yourself
3. **Integrity** - "soundness of character"; living by right beliefs

QUESTIONS FOR REVIEW

Ask as you review each Word of the Week:

- Who can tell me what _____ is?
- Why is it important?
- How can we practice it in our daily lives?

21

INTEGRATING THESE WORDS OF THE WEEK INTO YOUR CURRICULUM

USING WORDS OF THE WEEK AT RANK TESTING TIME

I t may suit your purposes to use Words of the Week during rank tests. For example, in my studios each black belt candidate is required to write an essay about what it means to be a black belt. They're also required to keep a note book starting at the intermediate level, in order to chart their progress toward black belt.

I provide a hand out to my students for their notebook that lists every word of the week as listed below, and I also provide my students with a student handbook that includes the same information (feel free to do the same):

1. **Courtesy** - "formal politeness"; to be shown to others at all times
2. **Growth** - "to flourish"; remain humble enough to always keep improving
3. **Courage** - "valor"; not the absence of fear, but going on in spite of fear

4. **Sincerity** - "being genuine"; mean what you say and do what you mean

5. **Honesty** - "being truthful"; always seek to do what is right

6. **Obedience** - "a sense of duty"; fulfilling obligations and following the rules

7. **Humility** - "freedom from pride"; avoid becoming foolishly over-confident

8. **Perseverance** - "to persist"; have a "never give up" attitude

9. **Honor** - "a sense of right and truth"; know right from wrong and do right

10. **Loyalty** - "faithfulness"; being true to others and what is right

11. **Self-control** - "handling your actions properly"; right action at all times

12. **Knowledge** - "that which is known"; applied knowledge is power

13. **Respect** - "esteem"; give it to others, earn it for yourself

14. **Integrity** - "soundness of character"; living by right beliefs

Testing Tips

Several months before each black belt test, I remind students that I will quiz them on what they've learned about the Words of the Week that we've discussed repeatedly over the last few years, and that they should review them before their exam. It's amazing to me how much these kids retain after learning these lessons and repeating them several times.

I also sometimes will ask students who are testing for lower ranks about a particular word of the week that we had covered during the previous month. I don't ever fail a student if they can't remember; instead, I use this as a way to reinforce the lessons we've been learning during our mat chats.

If you decide to use these lessons in your belt rank exams, just be certain to make it a positive experience by reassuring students who may get nervous and forget a word. Gently remind them and encourage them no matter how they respond. Remember, you want them to associate these lessons with positive memories as a way to anchor the life lessons you're teaching them to positive emotional experiences.

BONUS SECTION ON TEACHING CHILDREN

Modern teaching methods in the martial arts were pioneered by some of the more successful school owners I the U.S. and abroad. Over the next few pages I am going to list and explain some of the techniques that I've gleaned from successful school owners that have worked well for me in my own studios, along with those that I've developed myself over the years. I strongly suggest that you start using these methods in your classes to more effectively motivate your child-age students (although they work just as well for all age groups).

Tell-Show-Do

This is something I started doing after studying pedagogy in university, and it works so well I have since taught this technique to all my staff members over the years.

Tell-Show-Do is a way of integrating all five major learning styles (structured, sociological, auditory, visual, and tactile) into every class. In Tell-Show-Do, you first use a spoken instructional sequence for the auditory learners, and then you demonstrate the movement for the visual learners, followed by solo practice for the tactile learners, and finally integrating sequential practice and partnered practice for structured and sociological learners.

In this manner, you are addressing individuality in learning styles and making sure that each and every student is able to absorb the information and curriculum.

Vocalization and Engagement

You must speak clearly and project your voice to everyone in the room. It is important that you find your "command voice" and that you use it. The command voice is not yelling, but a projected speaking voice that reaches all corners of the teaching area. It is also important that you engage every student during instruction, taking care to avoid focusing on just one part of the class or a single student.

Some mistakes to avoid in vocalization and engagement are:

- Talking at the wall or away from the students. Always face the students or turn your head toward them when giving commands.
- Talking at the floor. Keep your head level when addressing the class.
- Not making eye contact. You should frequently make eye contact with your students when teaching class.
- Teaching to the center or the front of the room

only. You should walk around and circulate to every area of the room. And that leads me to the next teaching technique...

Praise-Correct-Praise (PCP)

This one is an old standby that isn't really discussed much nowadays, probably because it's been taken for granted that everyone knows it. PCP involves being a "good finder," always finding something positive about what the student is doing.

Specifically, you start by first pointing out a positive and desired behavior a student is exhibiting; next giving correction where needed; and then ending the interaction with more praise. For example:

- "Great front stance, Jimmy, I like the way you are bending that knee – nice and deep! Now, let's just chamber that fist a little higher, above the belt. That's it, excellent! That's the way a Black Belt does it!"

It is important when using PCP that the praise you give is genuine, that you only correct one major error in each interaction, and that you always end the interaction on a high note.

Positive Reframing

Positive reframing is simply avoiding the use of negatives when giving instructions. For instance, if you want a class to kick higher, instead of stating, "I don't want to see anyone kicking below their belts" you would say, "Okay everyone, I want to see every kick go as high as you can get it!"

Positively worded phrases send the proper message to the student, which is that we want them to succeed, and we are here to help them do so. Negative phrases will make the student feel as if they are failing, so always use Positive Reframing when giving instruction or directions.

Disguising Repetition

I like to say that repetition is the mother of all skill, but it is also the father of boredom and dropouts. Disguising repetition is perhaps the most important thing you can do to keep your classes interesting and engaging. When it comes to disguising repetition, I only have two words for you: Be creative! Try to change the way you teach a skill every time you teach it, especially after the students have the acquired the basics of a particular movement or technique.

Examples of ways to disguise repetition are:

- Using combinations
- Adding jumping and spinning to a move
- Using props (pads, bags, and targets)
- Balancing on one foot
- Multiple target combos (multiple props)
- Jumping over an obstacle before, during, or after performing a technique
- Partner drills and practice
- Blindfolded training
- Doing moves in reverse order

Walking the Lines

Walking the lines is a great way to ensure that you make individual contact with every single student in every single class. This personal attention will go a long way toward showing your students that you care. Your goal is to engage each student with eye contact and PCP at least three times in every single class. To do this, you have to walk the lines at least once every fifteen minutes or so. Spend no more than 15-30 seconds with each student, use PCP, and end each contact and interaction on a high note.

No Downtime

No downtime means that you keep the class moving at all times, never letting the action stop. For adults, this is usually pretty easy, but with kids it can be a challenge.

Some suggestions:

- Make your explanations as short and concise as possible. Avoid giving long-winded explanations of technique.
- Change things up a lot. For adults and teens, change the pace every five minutes or so. For kids 7-12, change things up about every three minutes. For age 6 and under, change things every 1-2 minutes (yes, you will be worn out after your kid's classes).
- Save verbal history lessons for break time; Q & A sessions and mat chats should be saved for the end of each class.

Use a Written Lesson Plan for Every Single Class

Don't even think about stepping out on the floor without a written lesson plan. Lesson plans keep you on track and they help you ensure that you are covering the necessary curriculum for any upcoming exams. I have included a template for writing lesson plans on the next page; photocopy it and use it religiously. Better yet, type your lesson plans in your word processor for each class and rank level and save them on your computer's hard drive and back them up to disk. Then at the end of the year, you'll never have to write another one again.

Massie's Martial Arts
Instructor Training Program
Lesson Plan Worksheet

Warm-up ____ min: _____

Basics ____ min: _____

Break ____ min.

Pad Drills ____ min: _____

Self-Defense ____ min: _____

Variety Segment ____ min: _____

Fun Drill ____ min: _____

ABOUT THE AUTHOR

Mike Massie is the author of the *Martial Arts Character Education Lesson Plans for Children*, *Small Dojo Big Profits*, and over a dozen other martial arts business books and courses.

Mr. Massie has been a professional martial arts instructor since the early 90s. He holds dan ranks in Moo Duk Kwan, Tae Kwon Do, Hapkido, and Shotokan karate, and has been studying and training in the martial arts since the mid-80s.

Through his manuals, blog, and business coaching program, Mr. Massie has helped thousands of martial artists achieve greater financial success while finding increased personal satisfaction in their careers as professional instructors.

Mr. Massie lives with his family in Austin, Texas.

For information regarding Mr. Massie's business coaching services, visit:

DojoSuccessCoach.com

Made in the USA
Columbia, SC
17 November 2021

49165777R00062